Origins

Ant's Bug Adventure

Jan Burchett and Sara Vogler ■ Jonatronix

OXFORD
UNIVERSITY PRESS

In this story

Ant

Ant's dad

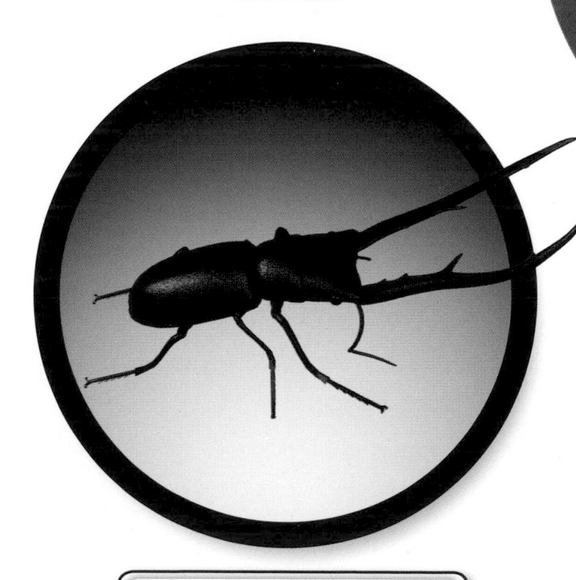

Stag beetle

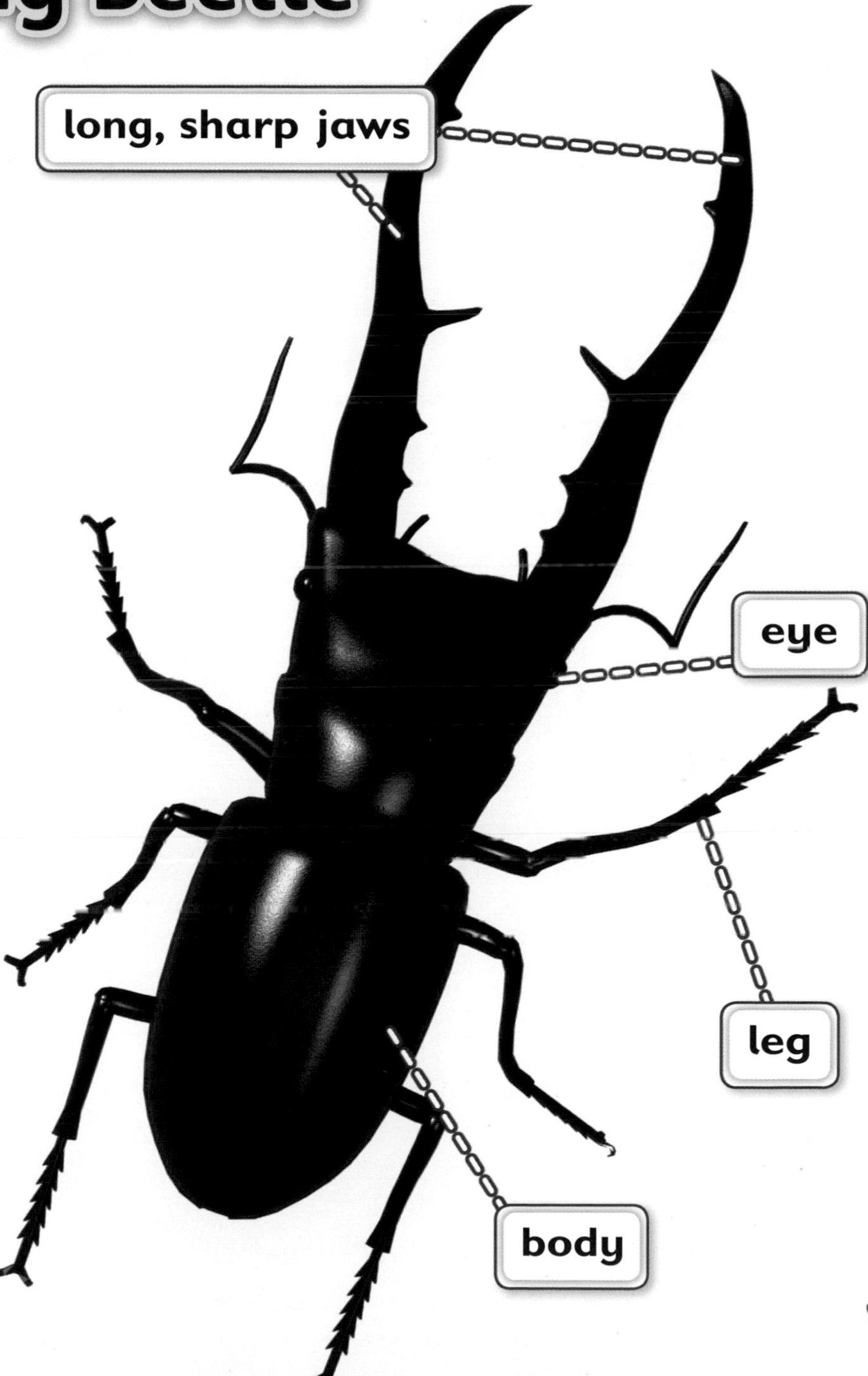

long, sharp jaws

eye

leg

body

Ant and his dad were on a walk. Dad had stopped to talk.

Ant was bored. Then he saw a hollow log.

Ant looked inside the log but it was dark.

"I will see more if I am small ..." he said.

He pushed the button …

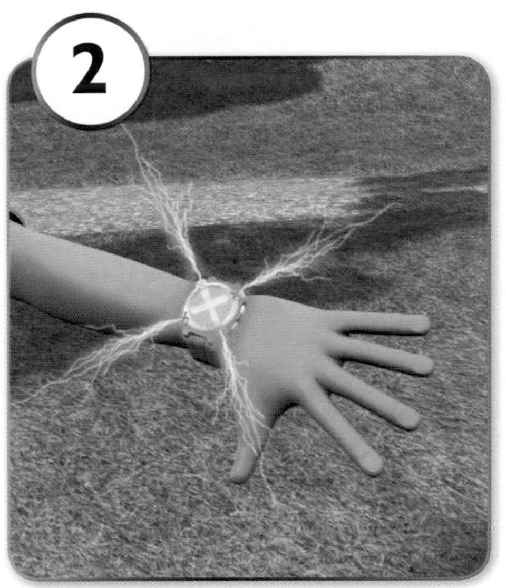

The log was full of bugs.
Cool!

Suddenly the log shook. Ant saw a big, dark shape. It was a stag beetle.

The beetle was black with
big jaws.
"Wow!" said Ant. "I will take a
photo with my watch."

Flash! went the watch.
The flash made the beetle jump.
It ran at Ant!

“Help!” yelled Ant.
He ran as fast as he could.
The beetle ran faster.

Ant found a small hole. He jumped out and landed on the ground.

Ant pushed the button …

He picked up the stag beetle.
"Not so scary now!" he said.

After reading

Talk with your child about the book. Here are some questions you could ask:

- Why did Ant look in the log?
- What did he do then?
- What did you think was funny about the story?
- How did the book make you feel?

Encourage your child to read the story again. This will build their reading confidence and reading fluency.

Other things to do

Keep talking about this book.

Find out more about stag beetles and other bugs using library books and the Internet.

OXFORD
UNIVERSITY PRESS
Great Clarendon Street, Oxford, OX2 6DP,
United Kingdom

Oxford University Press is a department of the University of Oxford.
It furthers the University's objective of excellence in research, scholarship,
and education by publishing worldwide. Oxford is a registered trade mark of
Oxford University Press in the UK and in certain other countries

First Edition published in 2009
This Edition published in 2014

British Library Cataloguing in Publication Data
Data available

978-0-19-830430-2

10

Paper used in the production of this book is a natural, recyclable product made from wood grown in sustainable forests. The manufacturing process conforms to the environmental regulations of the country of origin.

Printed in China by Leo Paper Products Ltd.

Acknowledgements

Illustrations by Jonatronix Ltd

Project X concept by Rod Theodorou and Emma Lynch

Lead Author of the Project X Character books: Tony Bradman

Origins

Book Band 4
Light Blue

Oxford
Level 4

Letters and Sounds
Phase 4

Ant's Bug Adventure

What will Ant find in the log?

Great for Guided Reading

Titles on the theme: ***Bugs***

The Race (Fiction)
> **Ant's Bug Adventure** (Fiction)
Zak and Zee (Fiction)
Bug Hunt (Non-fiction)
What Do Bugs Eat? (Non-fiction)

OXFORD
UNIVERSITY PRESS

How to get in touch:
web www.oxfordprimary.co.uk
email schools.enquiries.uk@oup.com
tel. +44 (0) 1536 452610
fax +44 (0) 1865 313472

ISBN 978-0-19